LEADERS
Create the Environment

Dave,
Hope you like it

Tom

T H O M A S   G U T H R I E

PAGE PUBLISHING, INC.
Conneaut Lake, PA

First originally published by Page Publishing 2020

ISBN 978-1-64701-282-3 (pbk)
ISBN 978-1-64701-283-0 (digital)

Printed in the United States of America

INTRODUCTION

If I do this correctly, this book is for the leader/practitioner more than for the academic leadership theorist. This book attempts to tie together many components that make up organizations: values, climate, culture, organizational physics, building trust, empowering the people in the organization, and setting the organizational environment.

I have always found all these topics very interesting; and over the course of a twenty-eight-year Army career, followed by my "life number 2," facilitating discussions on these topics, I have seen good, great, and poor organizations and often opined to myself, "Why would a leader accept being in a poor-performing organization?"

One disclaimer: in outlining this book, I envision something in the neighborhood of one-hundred-plus pages, but being concise is one of my more prevalent genes, so I am betting now that it will end up being half of that.

ACKNOWLEDGMENTS

I truly want to thank my wife, Kim, for twenty-nine years of marriage, two wonderful kids, and her support. It is not easy being the spouse of someone in the Army. Twenty-three of those years spent together were in the Army where we moved thirteen times. That is a ton of packing and unpacking. Every move brings with it new schools to register the kids for, new clinics for medical care, and many other things. Kim is a great wife, a great mother, and even a better person. When I grow up, I hope to be like her.

I also want to thank a friend of mine from the Kansas City area, Michael Sommers, for getting me off my butt and putting these thoughts on paper. Thanks, Michael.

$$E = f\,(Values + Climate + Culture)$$

CHAPTER 1

Organizational Values

I submit that every organization possesses organizational values whether officially stated or not. Corporations big and small, the horse ranch, sports teams, military units, social clubs, and even families all have them. In my experience, successful organizations spell those values out for all to see, and the less successful ones, or even poor ones, tend not to do so.

I cannot lie—growing up the son of a career US Army officer, our family did not have our organizational values inscribed anywhere, but they are pretty easy to recall: *love, competition, toughness, standards, and uphold the family reputation* were the pillars of our "unit."

As a young boy, I cannot recall any of the houses that we lived in during the frequent moves that did not have a basement that was set up for competition. A miniature basketball hoop with steel rim and Plexiglas backboard, dartboard, pool table, ping-pong table, and that old floor-hockey game with the push-pull rods were all staples of the Guthrie house. The backyard was our baseball, whiffle ball, and football field outfitted with plastic bases. The driveway had a basketball hoop mounted above the garage door, and the driveway also served as a great street-hockey rink.

What made this environment somewhat unique was that neither myself nor my little brother *ever* beat my dad until we earned it. Ever. Letting me win a simple game of floor hockey when I was seven years old was simply not permitted. What was permitted was my dad informing me that, "You lost again because your goalie sucks."

My mom was a little better, but not much. I distinctly remember being ten years old and fancying myself to be quite the basketball player. I would spend hours shooting, dribbling between my legs, and spinning the ball on my fingers like a Harlem globe-trotter (in my mind, at least). I challenged my five-foot-tall mom to a game of *horse* one day… That was the day I found out that Mom was a shooting guard for The College of William & Mary as she rained these ridiculous-looking, but incredibly accurate, two-handed set shots from deep behind the arc. That was the day I committed myself to focusing on beating my little brother, eight years my junior, at everything for years to come.

Standards and commitment. You learned early about personal responsibility in my house. If you said that you were going to do something, it was as if it was written in stone. Again, when I was ten years old, I desperately wanted to play football. My dad's deal was that if I weighed at least one hundred pounds when practices started, then I could play.

I stuffed loaves of bread down my throat and gallons of milk that summer but came up short. Doing nothing over the course of the fall season was never an option in our family, so I chose to play soccer primarily because it was the only other sport available.

Now, I was a good athlete, but even I knew after a week of practice that I was a horrible soccer player. Horrible. I came home after a Friday practice and announced at dinner that I was quitting. Five minutes later and after hearing the phrases, "Guthries keep their word and promises," and "Guthrie's don't quit anything ever," about six times each, I learned that commitment was a pretty big deal in this family. And although I remained horrible at soccer, I did finish the season.

My family's values do not fall far from the tree, but do take into account my wife of twenty-nine years, Kim's, personality. I would likely replace *toughness* with "productivity" and slightly amend *uphold the family reputation* with "Don't embarrass the family."

Sitting around all day in your pajamas is not something that occurs in my family. Kim is not only a physical therapist assistant but also a fitness instructor certified in basically everything. No one is spared. My college-soccer-playing son and now serving in the elite US Army's 75th Ranger Regiment is a self-starter with regard to working out. My beautiful twenty-one year old daughter with cerebral palsy, Merrin, however, does not get a sympathy pass on moving her body every day. Resistance is futile as they say. A workout is a given, but that is not enough. "What else did you *do* today?" is a common question, and "Nothing" is an improper response.

Conducting yourself in accordance with the Guthrie "brand" is a pretty big deal in my house. As a career Army officer, I have commanded and led small formations with little budgets to very large formations with annual budgets well in excess of $500 mil. In those "more important" positions, there were countless times when I was required to make presentations, speeches, etc. Every time I left the house to do one of them, Kim would remind me, "Don't embarrass the family." It was a consistent reminder to me that you better check your ego at the door and also that we represent each other. All our actions and behaviors have an impact on the family name.

Army Values. The Army has seven core values codified and well known to everyone in the big green machine. These were very carefully crafted with the idea that every soldier in the Army must embrace and embody them. These values guide our behavior, as well as how its members will interact with each other.

Not so coincidently, the seven Army values, when arranged just so, spell the acronym LDRSHIP—leadership. When all the soldiers in any-size outfit live these values, powerful things happen. On occasion the public will hear that an Army leader got in trouble. Now those troubles may have legal ramifications, but I contend that regardless of the unfortunate behavior or action, you can trace that leader's failure to simply not adhering to all seven of the Army values.

Corporate Values?

What are the values of your organization? Your company? Your sports team? Your mom-and-pop shop? It is my opinion that if your organization, regardless of size or function, has employees, then you should have stated organizational values that govern collective and individual behavior. I look up companies on the Internet with some frequency, and nearly every one of them has a professional-looking website with tabs at the top labeled: Home, About Us, Careers, Leadership Team, Our Products/Services, etc. Very, very few of them lead with a "Corporate Values" tab.

I heard an executive admit that his company does have organizational values, but they don't publish them. Interesting. They keep them a secret for what compelling reason? I have no idea.

I recently was randomly surfing the web when I came across a company that has been making and selling avionic parts and electronics for over sixty years, and yet they say, "Although we make and sell these items, *what we really sell is our integrity, reliability, and trust.*" Perfect. The outcome of their corporate values is the profit they make, but that profit does not occur without the values embedded in their organization.

If a company does not have guiding values to anchor it, then what is the company for? I am capitalist at heart, but if the company only exists to provide a product or service for profit, then it makes me wonder how they go about doing that.

CHAPTER 2

Climate

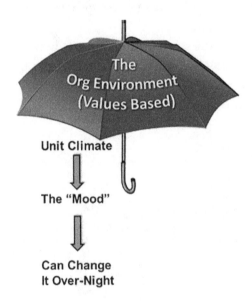

Senior leaders often use the words "culture" and "climate" as synonyms when describing what they need to change in their organization. They should not because those words are not synonyms.

If the climate is the mood of the organization, then a change in leadership can create a change in mood very, very quickly (for good or bad), depending on the leader's personality, competence level, values, and what that leader deems to be important.

My "bad mood" story:

It was the summer of 1989 at Ft Lewis, Washington, home of the 2nd Ranger Battalion, to which I was assigned. I had arrived to this battalion back in the early fall of 1987 as an infantry lieutenant, so by the summer of 1989 I was pretty experienced and confident in leading these Rangers.

As mentioned earlier, Rangers were back then, and remain today, a very elite fighting unit. Every member is handpicked, and every member goes through a rigorous selection process. No one just "joins" the Ranger Regiment. The regiment selects you and then "allows" you to serve in their ranks as long as you can meet or exceed all its physical and mental demands. Some say, and I would agree, that although getting into the Rangers is hard, it is almost as hard to stay. One slipup, one mild indiscretion, one violation can lead to you being handed your walking papers. It is not an organization for the timid and unsure.

With that as context, from 1987 to 1989 our battalion commander for that period was a very impressive leader. The commander of a battalion is a lieutenant colonel (LTC) with typically between seventeen to nineteen years of experience. Ours was a great one. Nothing is ever 100 percent, but I would say with great confidence that almost all the officers in the battalion wanted to "grow up and be very much like our battalion commander."

All good things come to an end. In the Army a battalion commander typically stays in command for two years before giving up command and moving to positions of greater responsibility. Such was the case in the summer of 1989. The change-of-command ceremony is a big deal. The entire battalion is formed and on display for the hundreds of guests. Speeches are made (usually a long one by the outgoing commander and a shorter one by the new commander).

Everything in the ceremony went according to plan. Our beloved outgoing battalion commander gave a great speech where he applauded the battalion for being (paraphrasing here) "the most lethal, devastating fighting force in the history of not just modern history but the entire history of warfare..." Hyperbole is fully authorized by the outgoing commander, but in truth, we believed it. The new commander did the right thing and kept his remarks short, and the ceremony concluded.

As is also typical following such a ceremony, the new commander schedules a time following the reception to talk to the leaders of the battalion. This is done mostly so that the new commander can give his subordinates a feeling of how he plans to lead this unit. This meeting is very common.

All the leaders, about forty of us, met in the dining facility at the appointed time. In walked our new commander, and consistent with Army protocol, we all stood up and came to the position of attention. He told us to relax, and we sat down. What followed was his first utterance to the leaders of the mighty 2nd Ranger Battalion: "Good afternoon, Rangers, I am LTC XXX, and this battalion is no better than any other unit in the Army. You just have better equipment and more funding."

Never pass up the opportunity to make a good first impression. Wow! In just ten seconds he changed the climate of that battalion from inspired and loyal to uninspired and angry. Several of us LTs had been contemplating extending our service in the battalion a few extra months before the Army would move us anyway. With that one sentence, all of us withdrew our paperwork.

To be fair, it is much easier to tell stories of leadership gone bad than it is to sing praises. Fact is, during a twenty-eight-year career, serving in twenty different jobs, I can say that I personally only had two bosses that I felt did not deserve to lead me. Interesting to me is that they both had something in common: they both, intentionally or unintentionally, created a climate where their subordinates were there to serve them instead of a climate where they, as the leader, set conditions for their subordinates' success.

I firmly believe that the climate of an organization can change on the very first day of a new leader's arrival, so if true, why wouldn't leaders want it to be a positive experience? Leaders *own* the climate.

CHAPTER 3

Culture

Unit Culture

The Sum of the
Org's Habits

I believe that the culture of an organization includes its history, traditions, rituals, belief system, norms, and even its reputation.

Not all organizational cultures are the same. A nuclear power plant's culture might lean heavily on rules, processes, and regulations to govern individual and collective behavior. From my uninformed perspective regarding nuclear energy, that seems perfectly understandable given the potential severity of mistakes.

Although the Army is tied together by their bond to the Army values, the Army is full of differing cultures. The previously mentioned Ranger Regiment is known for a culture built on discipline, mental and physical toughness, and expertise at small-unit tactics. In addition to the Army values, the Rangers have their own creed shown below, and this creed is not simply a PowerPoint slide on the wall of the headquarters. The words of the creed are spoken every morning before physical training, and this creed is internalized by every Ranger.

Ranger Creed

Recognizing that I volunteered as a Ranger, fully knowing the hazards of my chosen profession, I will always endeavor to uphold the prestige, honor, and high esprit de corps of the Rangers.

Acknowledging the fact that a Ranger is a more elite Soldier who arrives at the cutting edge of battle by land, sea, or air, I accept the fact that as a Ranger my country expects me to move further, faster and fight harder than any other Soldier.

Never shall I fail my comrades. I will always keep myself mentally alert, physically strong and morally straight and I will shoulder more than my share of the task whatever it may be, one-hundred-percent and then some.

Gallantly will I show the world that I am a specially selected and well-trained Soldier. My courtesy to superior officers, neatness of dress and care of equipment shall set the example for others to follow.

Energetically will I meet the enemies of my country. I shall defeat them on the field of battle for I am better trained and will fight with all my might. Surrender is not a Ranger word. I will never leave a fallen comrade to fall into the hands of the enemy and under no circumstances will I ever embarrass my country.

Readily will I display the intestinal fortitude required to fight on to the Ranger objective and complete the mission though I be the lone survivor.

Rangers lead the way!

The Armored Cavalry Regiments (ACRs) have a unique culture as well. I never served in one, but it is no secret that a "Cavalry Way" exists. The current ACRs possess incredible combat power with seemingly endless numbers of tanks and Bradley Fighting Vehicles, but their culture dates back to horseback warfare. The ACR culture is born from those early days: speed, audacity, flexibility, courage, and a certain panache are internalized by all cavalrymen.

Their traditions reflect that: the spur rides, where new members earn their spurs (literally a set of spurs); the Stetson ceremony, where Cavalry leaders earn their Stetson, which they wear during special ceremonies and events. I have never met a cavalryman who wasn't proud to show off his Stetson.

Google is widely known as a company that possesses a culture of creativity, innovation, and experimentation. Given that culture, I would be utterly shocked if the Google policies handbook (if they even have one) would state, "Employee creativity time is from 9:00–9:30 every other Tuesday."

Apple, under Steve Jobs, was known for having a culture of the same type of innovation but also one where Jobs expected people to do the impossible and then watched as they did.

Since the organizational culture, whether good or bad, precedes the new leader's arrival, it would be prudent for that leader to assess the culture before simply demanding that changes be made.

Even though I grew up in the Army in Ranger and light infantry cultures, I certainly hope that if the Army had asked me to lead a cavalry formation, then I would have been smart enough to embrace their "funny" tanker boots and spurs, the Stetson, and sing their cavalry songs with vigor. Leaders who attempt to change a pretty proud culture for personality reasons are typically doomed for failure.

CHAPTER 4

Organizational Environment

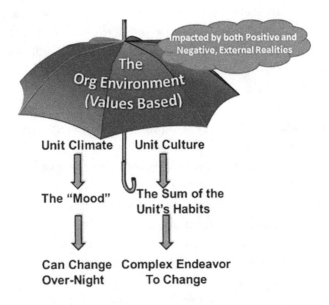

Regardless of good or bad (climate) or easy or hard to change (culture), the leader owns it all. *He/she owns the organizational environment.*

Assuming that an organization possesses a reasonably sound vision and has chartered a course to try to attain it (strategy/goals), all that might be needed to complete the recipe is an organizational environment that supports achieving those goals.

CEOs and senior leaders are typically good at creating and describing the vision for their organization. They appear equally deft at laying out a strategy that, if followed, will move the organization toward those goals. Not many—I think—are willing to, or confident enough to, describe to their workforce the organizational environment that will guide individual and collective behavior.

Vision + Strategy = The future and a plan (*The why, the what, and even the when in many cases*)

Organizational Environment = *The how—how people will interact with each other*

Consistency is the key, but it cannot be achieved if the leader has not outlined and described to the workforce (top to bottom) what that organizational environment looks like. When the audio (what we say) matches the video (what we actually do), it is powerful. Doing this (audio matching video) for a short period of time (days, weeks) will change the climate. Doing so for an extended period of time (years) will likely change the culture. The true measure of change is how well that change weathers individual arrivals and departures. If the organizational environment is tied to one person (or a small group of people), then it is unlikely to last.

I purposely used the umbrella in the graphic to illustrate that no matter how "perfect" your internal environment may be, there are outside influences that can affect it both positively and negatively. What does a leader do when his/her boss has a "different" environment in mind? Do they provide environmental shelter from the negative influences to their organization, or do they act like a sieve?

If the leader acts like a sieve, thus allowing the higher, external, and negative influence to affect his/her organization, then I contend that they have abdicated their leadership responsibility, and they are not even needed (the boss above you is also the boss of your people, so you become irrelevant). Figure a way to be that umbrella, and your people will go the extra mile for you. Leaders create the environment.

CHAPTER 5

Creating the Organizational Environment: An Example

All models have some utility, and very few are perfect. What I describe in the coming chapters was my conscious effort applied to what the organizational environment would look like and feel like when I headed into command of an infantry battalion (about seven hundred soldiers on any given day). Having spent sixteen years in such units, I was intimately familiar with the battalion's mission, its key tasks, etc. None of that was new to me.

I did not have an appreciation of this unit's history, which very much informed its culture. I commanded 2nd Battalion of the 27th Infantry Regiment—The Wolfhounds. That nickname was born in Siberia when the unit was fighting the Russians. The Russians were told to have said that "these men fight with the ferocity of wolfhounds." Pretty cool. They fought with consistent distinction through WWII, Korea, and Vietnam, having had more than a handful of Wolfhounds earning the Medal of Honor. This unit, like many across the Army, continues to deploy to Iraq and Afghanistan.

I was also unaware that a bond between Japan and the Wolfhounds had been formed back in the post-war Japan occupation—a bond between a Japanese orphanage in Osaka, Japan, and members of the unit that still existed in 2001 (and even today in

2020). A Sergeant Hugh O'Reilly, during the occupation of Japan, came across this orphanage and was so struck by the despair he personally began passing the hat among the Wolfhounds to raise money for the orphans' basic necessities (food, shelter, clothes).

That relationship exists today and is demonstrated twice a year. Each summer three to five orphans are selected to come to Hawaii, where the Regiment is located, and spend ten days doing all sorts of activities while living with various Wolfhound families.

Each winter two Wolfhound soldiers are selected (and it is very competitive) to serve as Secret Santa and are flown to Japan with literally hundreds of gifts provided by Wolfhound families to pass out to the kids at the orphanage. You can't make this stuff up if you tried, but all that affects the unit's culture and informed me greatly on my way into command.

With that as context, I penned after great thought what I wanted the organizational environment to look and feel like. I wanted these relatively simple ideas to govern how we would treat each other as we collectively move toward improving ourselves as individuals and as ground-fighting force with difficult missions. This framework, by the way, not only served me well in battalion command but remained virtually unchanged as I moved into brigade command (higher responsibility) and even as an Infantry Division chief of staff.

Create the Environment

- the knowledge that subordinate input is valued;
- leaders communicate, listen, and care;
- a sense of collaboration, shared responsibility, and trust exists;
- freedom to exercise initiative;
- honest mistakes are forgiven;
- role models and mentors are present and active;
- challenging education and training;

- organizational assignment opportunities that prepare leaders for future responsibilities are deliberately planned;
- employee and leader's time are not wasted;
- teamwork—downward, laterally, upward, and even with our competitors.

CHAPTER 6

The Knowledge that Subordinate Input is Valued

Huge in impact, so easy to implement and demonstrate, and yet often overlooked. Some leaders, even very senior leaders, feel that with their positional power and title comes all the good ideas and solutions. Some do not even ask for input. I assume because doing so might minimize their importance. That is all very silly. The benefits of inclusion are enormous. When people in any organization in any field of work know that their ideas and opinions matter, then they feel appreciated. And they will do more, not less.

The more senior you become in an organization, the less you should talk and the more you should listen. You may in fact already have *the* answer to a specific problem, but more than likely it just *an* answer. In my experience, if you let others bat the subject around and you just listen, if nothing else, you gain valuable perspectives as to how others view the problem, and you might just obtain additional clarity.

For those that are thinking that what I just described is "leadership by committee," then you missed the point. At some point a decision must be made, and that is typically up to the leader. A perfect illustration of this is what a former great boss of mine called *"Phase 1, Phase 2."*

He was a very seasoned senior commander, and I was his chief of staff, responsible in some ways for taking his vision and intent for this large formation and turning that vision and intent into action and results.

He described Phase 1 as a period of time where he needed and truly wanted a wide range of subordinate leaders' input, thoughts, ideas, and opinions on the topic/problem at hand. Depending on the complexity of the issue and/or the time available to make a decision, Phase 1 may last a week or more or as little as two hours. Phase 1 was open discourse, and no one was stifled; in fact, we were very much encouraged to voice our views.

At some point the boss had to transition to Phase 2. It might be that the time available had reached its end, or maybe he had heard enough varied opinions on the subject to now make a decision so that we could move forward. Phase 2 was decision time. He would publicly thank everyone for the Phase 1 input and told us that he valued all of it. He then offered his decision.

Now with upward of ten leaders involved in a hypothetical Phase 1 discussion, there might be one to two that "won" because their solution was accepted; but because the other eight to nine of us were able to participate in the process, none of us ever left that meeting feeling like we had "lost." The beauty of this process was in its simplicity. Since we all played a valued role in Phase 1, none us ever wasted additional energy after the Phase 2 decision, trying to get the boss to "reconsider." Everyone on the team put both oars in the water and rowed to the Phase 2 edict.

CHAPTER 7

Leaders Communicate, Listen, and Care

*The older I get, the more I listen because if I do not,
then I remain trapped in my own experiences.*

—A retired general, circa 2011

I absolutely love this quote, and I was able to hear it firsthand while attending a conference where many young Army leaders were gathered to pass along their perspectives regarding the health of the Army as a profession after so many years of persistent conflict (at that time, about a decade's worth).

Young leader after next described their perception of the Army profession, and not all their remarks were flattering. I was an "old" Army colonel at the time, and even though I consider myself to be a very patient person, admittedly it was all I could do to refrain from grabbing the microphone and "setting those young, inexperienced, and obviously uninformed leaders straight."

Then I overhead the retired general lean over and whisper this quote to a colleague who was in attendance, and I immediately knew that he was right. He could have at any point, concisely and with great historical and experiential credibility, shut down the entire discussion with a one-to-two-minute soliloquy. He did not. He did not because he was there not to preach or to lecture but to *learn* how others viewed that topic so that he could be better informed. To that end, here is my simple "Talk or Listen" scale:

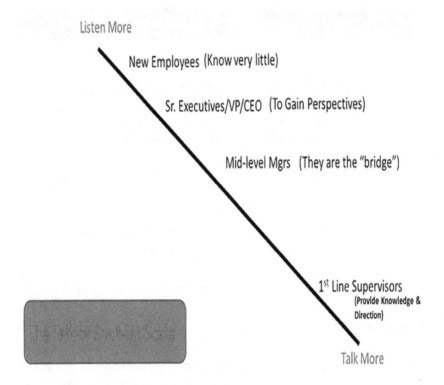

The lesson learned from that short story is that the word "communicating" often becomes a synonym for "talking" when viewed from the perspective of senior leadership. It is almost as if they believe that if they are not talking, then they are not doing their job. Communicating is a two-way street. Both or multiple parties get a chance to speak and listen.

The more senior you get in an organization, the more opportunity you have to simply *talk at* people instead of *talking with* them. There is a huge difference, and it is immediately noticeable which type of leader you are. Subordinates want a dialogue with their leaders not a constant stream of monologues.

Leaders communicate, listen, and *care*. If the word *care* conjures up some fuzzy feeling where everyone in the organization is due one hug a day, then please stop. Most of us can tell almost immediately if a leader truly cares about the organization and its people or if the leader treats the people in it like cogs in a machine. If you treat people like the latter, you typically only achieve compliance—employees doing the bare minimum. When you treat them like valued members of the team where their contributions are appreciated, you typically achieve commitment—employees going above and beyond what is required.

CHAPTER 8

A Sense of Collaboration, Shared Responsibility, and Trust Exists

Let's start with trust since I believe it is the foundation for any successful organization. There is no shortage of books written on this topic, and I will take it as fact that organizations with high levels of trust outperform, outproduce, and have higher levels of return on investment than those organizations lacking trust. I believe there is a roadmap to building mutual trust.

Sometimes we are hired as an apprentice, the boss knowing full well that he/she will have to teach and train us for the job at hand. As a sixteen-year-old high-school junior working on Day 1 at a construction site, the on-site boss quickly realized my limited skill set, and so I was *trusted* only enough to "carry stuff" for the first four weeks.

As we get older, we are often hired (or not) based simply on our education, training, and experiences matching the specific job description: four years advertising experience and a master's degree, etc. In this case, it is reasonable to assume that the boss expects us to know what we are doing upon arrival and hit the ground running.

If you really want to end up *trusting* the new worker, regardless if he is a high-school kid doing summer work or your next Senior VP, follow a simple methodology passed to me and several others by the late, great General Wayne A. Downing back in 1988 when I was a young leader just starting my leadership journey.

He said (paraphrasing), "As a boss, every time you inherit or hire a "new" guy, regardless of age, rank, experience, or resume, follow this simple six-step process: A, T, T, V, A, T."

Assess: Assess the person's capabilities, knowledge, skills, and desire for the job he/she is about to be assigned. Depending on that assessment, the remainder of the steps in this process can occur quickly or somewhat slowly. Remember, however, the goal is to *trust* them at the end of the process.

Teach: Whatever educational gaps the person may have for their soon-to-be assigned position, those gaps must be filled *before* you assign them that role. Provide them that education.

Train: Once educated for the position, can they repeat the tasks required of it efficiently and reliably? This is very important for any job in the psychomotor realm. Provide them that training.

Validation: Once educated and trained, somebody in the organization must validate the person to perform the task(s) associated with the job to a pre-determined standard. Once validated,

Assign Responsibility: It is their job now. They know what to do, they know how to do it, and they can do it to standard. They have a clear understanding that they will now be held accountable for their piece of the larger organization.

Leaders who skip the previous steps in the process and go directly to Assigning Responsibility typically find themselves spending extra personal energy making a lot of corrections because they do not trust that person do either do their task right or to do the right thing. If the process is followed, and if they do the job well over a period of time, people in the organization, as well as the boss, begin to *trust them.*

And let us not forget that the trust process works both ways with a slight twist. The subordinate is also determining whether you, the boss, are trustworthy: Do you intend to teach and train them for the job? Do you possess competence and character? Do you hold yourself accountable, or only those that work for you? Do you care about the employees and the company or not?

Establishing mutual trust throughout the depth and breadth of the organization is the stepping stone to building a sense of shared responsibility in it. It is a lonely and tiring life if the leader is the only one in the organization who cares about its future. When everyone feels a vested interest in the success of the organization, it is powerful, and the boss can actually go home for dinner knowing that the wheels will continue turning.

The opportunity for the members to collaborate, to have their opinions voiced and listened to is the secret sauce that helps magnify that sense of shared responsibility. Collaboration does not mean that everything is discussed and then to put to a majority vote. Not even close. Leaders are there to make some tough decisions, but collaboration allows for additional information to be heard. When possible, if a decision is going to affect someone downstream, is there a way to involve them in the upstream process?

CHAPTER 9

Freedom to Exercise Initiative

Flattening an organization is not about speed and technology, it's about empowering members to exercise initiative.

For the past few years it appears to me that senior executives—whether they reside in business, politics, the military, or even athletics—all state a desire (a need) to "flatten their organization." "Flat" has evidently become synonymous with "better," but what is "flat," and under what conditions would flat be "better"? There is no shortage of articles written on this subject, and some of them are very well researched. Since I am lazy, I will skip the research effort, but I do listen actively for context.

Most bureaucracies have a hierarchical structure associated with them (see example below). Regardless of field (business, politics, etc.), the CEO at some point gets frustrated with the layering, the processes, the difficulty with getting *real* information, the perceived "slowness" of this structure, and therefore demands that the organization be *flattened.*

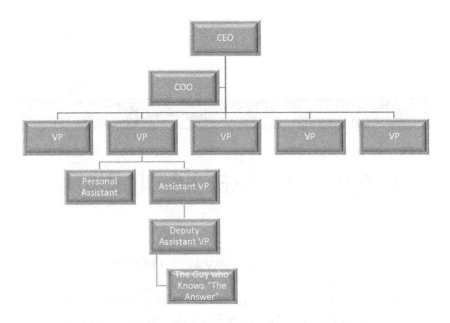

Given this very common scenario, the context for which the senior executives are using "flatten the organization" is really one of "accelerating the decision-making process." If true and with this as the context, CEOs seek to streamline the organizational structure by making it look physically flatter (it becomes visually wider and less deep). Their version of flat has almost nothing to with empowering subordinates, or creating an environment where taking the initiative is expected.

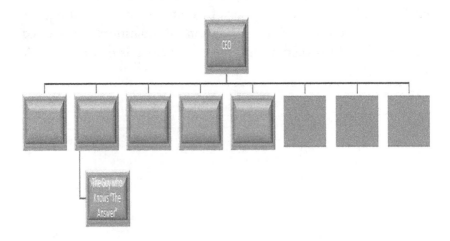

Whether intended or not, such a revised structure brings with it consequences. With a larger span of control, the CEO will undoubtedly have more meetings requiring his/her presence; he/she will probably receive more information that has not yet been vetted or questioned; and he/she will likely make more decisions per day, week, and month in this structure than he/she ever did previously. The CEOs will also feel the need to leverage technology and establish an organizational SharePoint site or company intranet that provides everyone the illusion of collaboration. *Bingo!* The CEO got what he/she wanted (a flatter organization) and in the process lost his/her longstanding Thursday 1:00 p.m. tee time at the club.

These CEOs got it (flat) wrong. "Flat" to them meant "faster" and, more specifically, the perceived *need* for them *to make decisions faster.*

The successful, fast, and flat organizations that I have seen and been a part of do not grade their "flatness" in terms of speed or the number of decisions that the "boss was able to make today." Quite the opposite. Regardless of what the organizational structure looked like on paper, the successful organizations knew *the power of "flat" meant moving the appropriate decision-making authority to where the knowledge actually resides (and hint: it is almost never at the top).* The guy who knows the answer (the bottom box below) is *empowered* (dare I say expected) to make the decision, consistent with the CEO's intent, so that the CEO doesn't have to be the one making it.

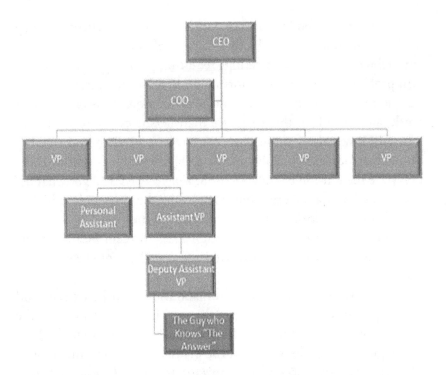

It is not the structure of the organization, or necessarily the processes that control it that matter, but it is the organizational environment that the leader creates which governs how the people in the organization, top to bottom, interact with each other and the responsibilities/authorities vested in them at echelon that matters.

It may seem counterintuitive for senior executives to *not* make a bunch of daily decisions, but if they are making numerous ones, then their organization is "slow" by their own hand.

When trust and empowerment (freedom for initiative) are combined, the effects are great. Members of the organization go above and beyond their required duties and do so willingly. They want to make the impossible possible.

When I was a CPT in the 75th Ranger Regt in the early 1990s for about eighteen months, I had a very demanding job as a Plans and Exercise officer responsible for knowing and coordinating the war plans and all the training exercises conducted in both Europe and the Middle East. The hours were long, and there was a ton of travel, but there was also a lot of responsibility and autonomy that came with it.

The commander of the Regiment, a colonel, had a vision at the time to "make the Rangers known globally," and to that end he directed me to coordinate a trip to Europe, where he could visit with like outfits from allied nations. This colonel had boundless energy and drive: the seven-day-total trip in March 1992 would involve visiting five countries during that span (Norway, Germany, Belgium, England, and France). It was an exciting and fast-paced event.

On the long plane ride back to Fort Benning, Georgia, the commander told me to write some notes down regarding his thoughts on how to move forward with getting Rangers into Europe. All I had was an airplane napkin, and I scribbled the best I could. This is a picture of that napkin, which I still have today:

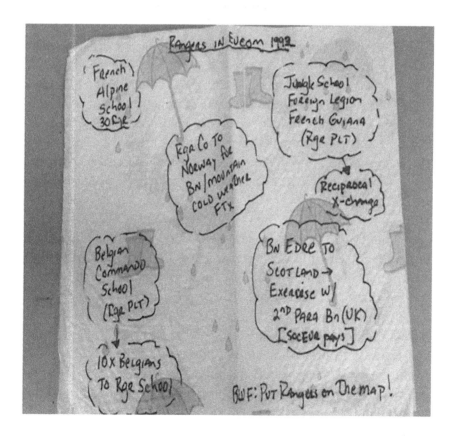

I will tell you that every one of these separate "clouds" constitutes a *ton* of work to coordinate.

- Thirty or so Rangers to attend the French Alpine School
- A Ranger platoon (thirty to forty Rangers) to attend the Belgian Commando School
- Coordinate for ten Belgian commandos to attend our US Army Ranger School (thank God for a thing called statute of limitations because I severely "bent" a few Army, and likely national, regulations making that one happen)
- A Ranger Company (approximately 150 Rangers) to Norway for a mountain-cold-weather exercise.
- Another Ranger platoon to attend the French Foreign Legion Jungle School in French Guinea, and in reciprocation, plan an exercise for forty legionnaires in the United States
- And the *big one!* Plan a "secret" Ranger battalion (seven hundred Rangers) exercise with the British Parachute Regiment where the Ranger Battalion would fly from Georgia to Scotland, conduct an airborne assault into Scotland, then plan a ten-day combined exercise with the Brits. Just to make that one more interesting, he told me that he did not want to pay for that exercise, so I needed to find some other headquarters to foot the near-$4million bill. Nice.

After he finished talking and me scribbling, I asked him my big question, knowing full well the amount of time and energy it would take to pull all of this off. I asked, "Sir, over what period of years do you see all of this happening?"

And his response was predictable. "Years? Screw that. I want all of this to happen before Christmas." Nine months of blood-sweat-and-tears staff work, we made the impossible possible. I keep that napkin as a reminder that when people trust you, empower you, and believe in you, you will do whatever it takes for the organization to be successful.

Honest Mistakes Are Forgiven

This is not a blanket statement that absolves even the biggest of screwups of all sin, but it is a simple acknowledgement that we all make mistakes, some big and many small.

I draw the distinction between making an honest one and one that is not by asking if this mistake was made in an effort to better the organization. If the mistake was one of commission and not of omission or negligence, then let's learn from it and move on. There is no loss of trust; it was simply a pretty good idea that unfortunately did not turn out the way the person intended.

Some leaders that I have seen and served with have a low tolerance for others' mistakes but appear perfectly fine with making some themselves.

Fixed or Free Energy?

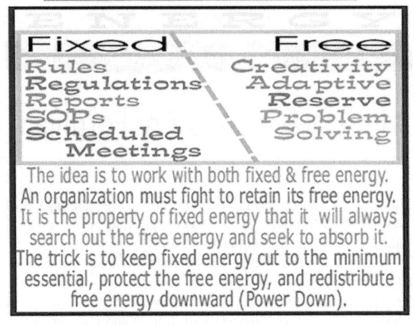

Fixed	Free
Rules	Creativity
Regulations	Adaptive
Reports	Reserve
SOPs	Problem
Scheduled	Solving
Meetings	

The idea is to work with both fixed & free energy. An organization must fight to retain its free energy. It is the property of fixed energy that it will always search out the free energy and seek to absorb it. The trick is to keep fixed energy cut to the minimum essential, protect the free energy, and redistribute free energy downward (Power Down).

Most organizations, to include the US Army, promote the desire for increased "free energy." Who wouldn't want a workforce that is creative, adaptive, and flexible? However, many leaders are reluctant to acknowledge that with that free energy comes the occasional failure. What they really want is bold, unconventional, creative people that stay within the organization's anal-retentive policies and processes, and that causes friction.

Leaders not comfortable with mistakes of commission tend to have knee-jerk reactions to relatively minor transgressions. If a subordinate makes a mistake, the boss simply removes that decision-making authority from that subordinate and places it at his/her level. No one learns anything when that is the solution. Fixed energy can swallow free energy if leaders are mistake averse.

CHAPTER 11

Role Models and Mentors Are Present and Active

Put simply, I believe completely in "lead by example." Leaders set the environment, and their actions, behaviors, and interactions have to be in alignment for the organization to succeed. Good leaders are always coaching, teaching, challenging, applauding, correcting, and developing their people. Not everyone will respond to your actions in the same way, and some will believe you are "great" while others may just see you as "average," but the goal of the leader at a minimum should be to serve as a good role model.

As I moved up in rank and position in the Army, we would occasionally get a briefing that would imply, "Be careful...as you get more senior, more people are watching you...you are now in a fishbowl." It always seemed to be framed negatively and as if senior leaders have the right to be somewhat paranoid. I don't buy into that one bit.

What an opportunity! If in fact everyone is watching you as a senior leader, what a great chance to serve as someone who is doing the right thing 24/7/365. It should be viewed as a gift instead of some burden.

I use the "mentor" in the tile of this chapter purposely because I think the word is often misused and overused. Some corporations and even the Army every so often consider *assigning* junior members of the organization a mentor, and I have never seen it work the way in which it was probably envisioned.

As I look back on twenty-eight years of service, I have come to the conclusion that being called a mentor by someone is, in my opinion, the highest honor any leader can receive.

As defined by Webster's Dictionary, a mentor is "someone who teaches or gives help and advice to a less experienced and often younger person."

Webster may have it right for the majority of Americans, but I offer one that I think is a bit better:

> *A mentor is someone who voluntarily provides professional and personal help and advice over time to a typically less-experienced person who is receptive and reciprocal in the exchange.*

I hope that every leader aspires to be viewed by their subordinates as a great teacher, coach, and role model, but it is the application of reciprocity and over the duration of time that separates those descriptors with that of being someone's mentor.

As an example, I commanded about forty to fifty officers between the rank of second lieutenant and major while I was in battalion command. I certainly hope that I was a good role model for all of them to emulate, and over the years I have continued to write letters of recommendation, assist them in getting one of their top three choices of assignments, etc. That said, upon leaving battalion command, I am very confident in saying that I was/still am a mentor for only about three of the lieutenants, two of the captains, and two of the majors. As a brigade commander, I added two lieutenant colonels and two majors. As a division chief of staff, I added two majors.

I can say all that with confidence because each has stayed in close personal and professional contact with me since that time. And I have reciprocated. When they call or write, it is not simply to ask for my help. Sometimes it is just an update on them and their family or often a need for some advice/counsel. If they don't write or call me for a while, I call or write them because it is personal, professional, and reciprocated over the long haul of life.

CHAPTER 12

Challenging Education and Training

This chapter is a predominately military/sports one, but hopefully there are some lessons to take away if you are in the business sector. I have seen some studies that show in any organization there is 25 percent of the workforce that goes above and beyond regardless of the reason why. They might just be passionate about their work, love the vision and direction, appreciate their coworkers, etc. These are *self-starters* who simply need some direction and support, and the leader needs to just get out of their way.

The massive middle group is estimated to be approximately 65 percent of the workforce. Many labels are associated with this group, but I like calling them the *Requirements* group. This sizeable group comes to work on time, and leaves on time. They do what is required in their job description and are typically uninterested in doing anything above that unless some form of compensation (money, time off, parking spot) is provided them. The leader has some choices for this group, and we will discuss those.

The last group is the remaining 10 percent, and I call them the *Oxygen Thief* group. They do less than what is required and hope that no one rats them out, they are "sick" seemingly all the time compared to other employees, and they typically are the ones who always have an ongoing official complaint being worked by somebody in HR.

Leaders don't have to inspire group 1 people; just let them be and applaud their efforts. Leaders should—or must, in my opinion—"encourage" the departure of group 3 members, hopefully using the least amount of personal and organizational energy as possible. I have always despised the phrase, "I spend 90 percent of my time on 10 percent of my people (group 3, no doubt)." That is a leadership choice, so why would you not be spending nearly 100 percent of your time focused on the 90 percent (groups 1 and 2) of your people?

So the question is, how do you move, or mobilize, group 2 (the majority) toward group 1 attitudes, behaviors, and actions? I suspect that the answer is not in having them attend briefings to "inform" them, or having a faceless employee development director point them to websites where they can gain "new knowledge," or even having a company sponsored Secret Santa Christmas party to prove how much you care about the employees.

This is hard stuff, and moving the entirety of the group 2 (65 percent) to group 1 is not possible, but as my father used to tell me when I was faced with something difficult, "Well, since it is hard, you gonna quit?" Reverse psychology tended to work on me.

I think organizations default to trying to move group 2 in a "collective" method because doing so is easier organizationally, and holding a seminar or having a knowledge website absolves those leaders from having to deal with this at the individual level. If Jake didn't go to the knowledge website, then that is his fault not mine. He had the opportunity to improve himself. I call that kind of leadership the Pontius Pilot leadership style: I wipe my hands of the matter.

So using a spin-off of my father's tactic, I recommend that leaders find a group 2 person and attempt to *iteratively* challenge them.

The boss: "John, do you have a minute?"

John: "Sure do."

The boss: "Great, I have a small problem that I need help with, and I think your specific skill set and talent can help solve it. This might stretch you a bit, but I am pretty confident that you can do it."

Bam! Trust, appreciation, request for help, and belief in John results in John saying yes.

What if John's response was, "No, thanks" or "Sure, but what's in it for me?"? In either case, the leader probably picked the wrong group 2 member to approach; but as the eternal optimist, let's assume John took on the task.

We must be cognizant that although this in an *individual* interaction, there are a bunch of group 2 people watching this from the sidelines. The leader should support John, coach him along the way, and give him tips and encouragement; but the leader cannot (a) tell him that "it is all f——ked up" on the back end of the task; or (b) take over the task at some point but try to pretend that John really was the one who did it. He needs to own this.

Doing (a) is traumatic to John, and as the leader, you just confirmed for John and the rest of group 2 that doing anything beyond just what is required is not worth the risk.

Doing (b) is disingenuous, and it would not go unnoticed by the group 2 people.

Back to optimism. John does well on his own. I recommend a short public form of recognition for John's work. Be a bit careful of overplaying this because you could create an expectation with the group 2 majority that they get "stuff" for just trying.

Just think of the organizational improvement you could make if you were able to move even a third of group 2 folks to the group 1 side: instead of 25/65/10 (normal organization as per the studies), you are now 46/44/10.

After nearly three decades of military, I believe that even most Army units are close to the 25/65/10 statistics. Most soldiers want a challenge, and I was no different. I chose to be in the infantry because it seemed to me to be a mentally and certainly physically challenging field. I wanted to be an airborne Ranger again because it was challenge within a challenge. While still in college, back in summer 1983, I had the opportunity to attend the three-week Airborne School at Fort Benning. I did too many push-ups to remember and got yelled at by the instructors constantly. At the end I graduated, and they pinned my "wings" on me. At nineteen years old I proclaimed myself an official "badass" for what I had just endured.

Fast forward to 1987 when I entered the two-month Ranger School. I wanted to complete Ranger School because (a) it was pretty much expected if you are going to be a successful infantry officer, and (b) you cannot even apply to become a member of the 75th Ranger Regiment without it.

Trust me when I tell you that just three days into the training and staring at fifty-five or so more days to go, I wished I was back at Airborne School, where it now looked comparatively like a vacation. Having virtually no sleep, only one army meal a day (MRE), and walking all day and night carrying and average of eighty pounds of gear over mountains, through deserts, and in swamps leads you to question your professional choices. And for people who go to the gym for a thirty-minute workout and take a shower, I was afforded three showers during that two-month span. It sucked. I entered Ranger School an incredibly fit 168 lbs. and graduated looking like a drowned rat at 129 lbs.

CPT Dan Allyn (right) pinning on my Ranger Tab

I hated it so much every morning I swore to myself that I would quit (and several do along the way). I obviously did not quit, but during the swamp phase in Florida on the sixth day of the ten-or-so day phase, up to my waist in swamp water, every minute of it I actually came up with a great plan in my now-delirious, food-starved brain. I would end this ridiculous adventure "honorably." I would be medically dropped.

Slugging through the swamp, I caught a glimpse out of my left rear periphery of two water moccasins swimming in the same direction of travel as me. Too tired to be afraid, I in fact saw my way out of this swamp and Ranger School. I slowly lowered my left arm off my rifle and put it in the water right in front of where the snakes would be swimming. Only one needed to bite, and I would be medically evacuated (a "honorable" way to fail), and I would have a lifetime factually based excuse for the rest of my life on why I didn't graduate Ranger School.

Those damn snakes just passed by my arm with no interest in biting me and clearly not knowing their role in the grand plan. I knew then that I would graduate. If you are incapable of having a snake bite you, then you deserve to be a Ranger. Being challenged to the brink of failure brings out the best in people.

Group 1 is self-motivated. Group 3 is unchallengeable. For your unique organization, find out what challenges the majority of group 2, but focus on the individual vice the collective.

CHAPTER 13

Organizational Assignments and Opportunities that Prepare Leaders for Future Responsibilities Are Deliberately Planned

Most of us have heard the adage, "Leaders create more leaders, not more followers," and it does have a nice sentiment attached to it. I do wonder though how many leaders truly embrace it instead of just saying it.

Back in early 2013, in my last job in the Army, I had the great privilege of serving as the director of Center for Army Leadership, where I was responsible for—guess—yes, Army leadership doctrine and leader development strategies. It was a great job.

At that very time my son was entering his second semester of his senior year in high school and was being recruited by several colleges to play soccer. I went on three or four of these visits because I had the time, and this was a big decision for him (and my wallet). Each trip was essentially the same. You show up to the designated building and room number, where you see many other athletes from all types of sports, as well as some family members. Someone from admissions goes over all kinds of administrative details, and at some point, each of them mentions in effect, "at (fill in the blank) University, we develop leaders…"

Now, me being me and sitting for the last nearly three years as the director of Center for Army Leadership, I cannot help myself.

I ask, "How?"

Their response was always, "How what?"

My follow up was, "How does this university develop them into leaders?"

Each would think for a bit then reply with, "Well, just being here in this wonderful university setting with great professors and facilities turns them into leaders."

At that point, I would end the intellectual attack, but the contention that just being there will turn them into leaders is hogwash. Just working at Google, or on a construction site, or even just being in the Army does not magically transform anyone into a leader.

In most developmental systems there are three components that typically need to be present: *intention, ownership and accountability.*

Intention speaks to the organization's desired outcome of the developmental process. "We want to develop leaders that (fill in the blank)." Using the university example, their response somewhat proved to me that there was no real intention. There was no plan or purpose. If your company, corporation, or sports team contends that leaders will be developed there, then start with filling in the blank in the sentence above.

Ownership speaks to the senior-level leaders of the organization establishing leader development as a priority not just in writing but in word, deed, and action. Ownership also speaks to the individuals within the organization being prepared and willing to develop.

Accountability also speaks on two levels: senior members are truly held accountable for how well they have developed those junior to them (subordinates), and individuals within the organization are held personally accountable for their own growth.

With that as a suitable framework, then the next question is, *how* will the organization develop their members? The Army describes leader development *as a continuous, progressive process whereby the syn-*

thesis of one's training, education, and experiences leads to growth over time. Development is accelerated when constructive and frequent counseling, peer relationships, and mentoring are present.

That description works for me, and let's expand the word leader to "people development." Not everyone in the organization needs, or even wants, to be a leader, but hopefully, we all want to grow. Now a CEO cannot possibly be personally responsible for every individual's development no more so than a US Army general can, but they can take on an appropriate cohort of subordinates to do so and can more importantly set an environment where they hold those subordinates accountable for developing their subordinates.

In this environment every leader, no matter how junior, is charged with developing a portion of their subordinates, and their superiors are held accountable for developing them. It is not that difficult. To make the idea even easier, I ask leaders at every echelon three basic questions:

Who is the target of your developmental efforts, the group that you will hold yourself accountable for?

What is the goal/end state for their development? The *intention:* "I want to develop these people/leaders so that at the end they (fill in the blank)."

Given that target and that intention, what activities or events will get each of them to that goal? What *training, education, and experiences* do I need to provide them to make that goal happen?

When leaders of organizations care enough to develop their subordinates and hold lower level leaders accountable for doing so as well, it is powerful.

CHAPTER 14

Employees' and Leaders' Time Is Not Wasted

By my own admission, I am obsessed with time, specifically not wasting it. I don't want my time wasted, but I equally do not want your time, or our time, or the organization's time to be wasted.

I am not the guy who says he will show up at your house "around" 6:00 p.m. I will tell you that I will show up *at* 6:15 p.m. And then I do. When I tell my family that dinner will be ready at 6:30 (I am the cook for our family), if you wander into the dining room at 6:40, then your potatoes and meat will be ten minutes colder than it would have been had you showed up on time. Yes, I am that guy.

The Army is actually really good at wasting time, and it always bothered me. The daily 6:00 a.m. battalion formation that precedes the sixty to ninety minutes of physical training is a great example. At the lowest unit level the squad (about eight to ten soldiers), feels compelled to be in position in preparation for their platoon's assembly. The platoon level leadership cannot possibly accept being the last platoon to be ready for their company's formation, which also refuses to be the last company in formation prior to the battalion formation. If left unchecked, it is perfectly common, and oftentimes expected, that the squad level units start all of this waste in forming up at 5:30 a.m. or earlier.

If you happen to be in airborne unit, which I was for about ten of my years in service, it borders on the absurd. For a relatively routine training jump that has the unit jumping out of the airplanes at 8:00 p.m., the following is the rough timeline, and it does not even include drawing your weapons, conducting refresher training, and some other things that all happen prior to this. And know that most of this activity typically occurs at the airfield, on the hot tarmac in spots like Fort Benning, Georgia, and Fort Bragg, North Carolina, in July:

12:30 p.m.: Formation to load busses/trucks
12:45 p.m.: Load busses/trucks
1:15 p.m.: Drive to the Airfield
2:00 p.m.: Assemble in chalk formation (essentially another formation)
2:30 p.m.: Draw parachutes
3:00 p.m.: Individuals put on parachutes
4:00 p.m.: All soldiers checked by a Jumpmaster
5:15 p.m.: Wait for the Air Force
6:15 p.m.: Load the aircraft and wait for an hour (why, I have no idea)
7:15 p.m.: Takeoff
8:00 p.m.: Jump

What is truly magnificent about this timeline is that you can go through all of it to include taking off and flying to the drop zone only to have the jump called off at 7:55 p.m. due to high winds. I made around 110 jumps in my time, and I am guessing another fifteen to twenty got called off. That's two to three weeks of my life that I cannot get back.

Time is truly money. I was an Infantry Division chief of staff, the leader of a very large (+/- 700), complex staff in Iraq from 2008–09. I tried to minimize the number of meetings so we could actually do work. We had one fairly large meeting a week where we would brief our commanding general (a wonderful leader). It was one of, if not the only, weekly meeting where he had to be present. For other less-important meetings, if he got pulled away or was going to be late, myself or another senior leader could press on and lead the meeting.

About sixty officers from the division staff descended on the conference room for the CG's brief. Unfortunately, my CG happened to be having an office call with his boss, a higher-ranking general, and it was going late. We all just waited. I could not let the staff leave because our CG could be walking into the room in the next five, seven, fifteen minutes.

With time on my hands, I did some beer-math. I looked around the room and counted the rough number of officers by rank in the room (colonels, lieutenant colonels, majors, captains). Knowing their approximate monthly pay and breaking it down into an "hourly rate", when we started the briefing forty-five minutes late, it was a loss of $25,000. And we should double that to $50K since they could have been working during that time but were unable to.

I subscribe to the "don't be late for me because I won't be late for you" theory, and I kept that philosophy even when I was in much senior positions. As a colonel in the Army, you typically hold pretty important and oftentimes demanding positions. That fact should not give you carte blanche to have people waiting for you. Doing so, stated or not, makes it seem like you believe that your time is more important than others'.

Why do some CEOs or people in other powerful positions intentionally make people wait for them? I have seen this tactic used, and I am convinced those that do it do so out of some perverse method of control. How petty.

Wasting people's time by showing up late is but one way to do so. Having meetings, sometimes lengthy ones, that have no tangible output is another common way to disrespect people's time. I resist having meetings unless:

- there is a stated purpose
- an agenda
- a timeline
- attendees listed

The only meetings I wanted to attend were the ones that had the purpose of getting the boss' guidance before moving forward, or ones that had the purpose of getting the boss' decision. I would try to avoid any meeting that was "an update," or "for everyone's information." Those are mostly unnecessary meetings and better suited for an e-mail or hung on some organizational shared drive.

Easy check: If you chair a meeting (meaning you are the boss of the meeting), at the end of the first one, ask everyone in attendance to physically show you the notes that they took over the course of the meeting. Undoubtedly some will have written/typed absolutely nothing down. Don't look at that as their professional failure or lack of attention.

Tell them not to come next time and remain doing something productive because clearly this meeting is of no value to that person or those people. I have done exactly this at many levels of leadership, and the bottom line is that I noticed that people come to meetings out of habit more so than because they get something out of it.

CHAPTER 15

Teamwork—Downward, Laterally, Upward, and Even with Our Competitors

If the leader of any organization has built it on a foundation of trust and then empowers the members in it to the point where a sense of shared responsibility exists, then teamwork will naturally follow. As a former boss of mine was fond of saying, "You have got to play well on three teams."

Team 1 is your team, the one you are responsible for. There is nothing egotistical about wanting your team to be the very best it can be. You are the leader of that team, so you get to create the organizational environment that will make it and the members in it successful.

Team 2 is the peer team (aka the competition in many cases). Whether it is 1st, 2nd, and 3rd Battalions within a US Army brigade, or Marketing, Manufacturing, and the Logistics teams within the larger company, peer teams exist; and if the larger organization intends to be successful, working in harmony is essential. Perfect harmony is fiction since we are human beings. 1st battalion beats 2nd and 3rd battalions during the sports-day competition. Marketing crushed the Logistics team at the company chili cook-off.

Competition is very healthy for the most part, but when peer competition starts to affect the larger organization negatively, it must be dealt with swiftly. If the annual bonuses for the Manufacturing team rests on their ability to increase production by 28 percent during the last three months of the year, then it is quite possible that the leader of that team makes some decisions that get them there. Unfortunately, in this situation, doing so will knowingly screw the Logistics team out of their bonuses because with finite transportation assets to move the product, the increase in production means that the Logistics team will get penalized for having product stockpiled in the warehouse.

You can tell a lot about a leader when they are put in positions where they may have to sacrifice some of their resources for the good of a peer. Play well on Team 2.

Team 3 is the bigger team that your team is a part of. I have witnessed quite a few leaders in the Army get so focused on making Team 1 the very best they forget that they are part of their boss' team. When that happens, it rarely ends well. These leaders slowly come to the false conclusion that their higher headquarters are "stupid" or "out to get us," and when those feelings get manifested, dysfunction reigns.

Easy way to be a Team 3 hero: find out what your boss' organizational issues, problems, and concerns are and then apply some personal energy in helping him/her solve some of them...and do so objectively.

CONCLUSION

If you are sifting through books in Terminal A at the Atlanta Airport and you are like me, one who scans the introduction and summary of books to determine its worthiness, then just go ahead and buy this book. Hell, it probably costs close to $15.00, which is less than two airport beers, and hopefully, it will be time better spent. Leaders create the environment. What environment are you creating?

Tom Guthrie is a retired US Army infantry officer with twenty-eight years of service. He commanded units from company level to brigade and served as the chief of staff, 25th Infantry Division. His last job while in uniform was as the director of the Center for Army Leadership. He currently resides in Kansas City, Kansas.

CPSIA information can be obtained
at www.ICGtesting.com
Printed in the USA
FSHW020252110720
71627FS